Sweet

Gift
RECIPES
and many more

Your Promise of Success

Welcome to the world of Confident Cooking, created for you in
our test kitchen, where recipes are double-tested by our team
of home economists to achieve a high standard of success.

MURDOCH BOOKS®
Sydney • London • Vancouver • New York

Pretty Packaging

Eye-catching presentation will boost sales at your next fete, and adds a delightful personal touch to gift-giving.

The most attractive packaging is often the simplest: colourful wrapping paper with striking ribbons, or a theme created around the seaside or the bush. Inexpensive items and recyclable materials—old jars and bottles, brown paper and cardboard, flowers, shells, fabric, paper ribbon and doilies, raffia and interesting containers—can all be combined with wonderful effects.

Wrapping paper in a variety of colours and textures is the easiest way to package most items. Use brilliant shades of tissue paper, clear or coloured cellophane, or handmade grass and petal papers. Even newspaper can be used imaginatively, and glossy printed wraps (although expensive) are an option. Brown paper looks effective tied bon-bon style around sweets and secured with coloured jute or banana paper ribbon.

Personalise your wrapping paper: cover heavy paper with potato prints;

spray with metallic and coloured paints for a dappled effect; stencil, or decorate with stickers.

Try using crushed brown paper instead of the usual fabric jar covers; wind string over the top to create the look of a parcel and finish with a string tassel. To make the tassel, cut eight or ten similar lengths of string, knot together at the centre, then fold in half at this point and tie the lengths together again slightly lower than the top knot. Clip the base of the tassel so threads are the same length; tie to the jar with a string bow.

Paper doilies make ideal covers for jars. Use them to line boxes or plates, painted or plain, or use as a stencil.

Position the doily on the surface you wish to stencil (paper or fabric). Apply paint with a stencil brush, or spray it on. Allow to dry before lifting the doily

Crepe paper is a old decorating favourite—the bright colours and the texture help create

a sense of festivity. Use to make small bags. Cut square or rectangular shapes the same size from crepe paper, fold in half (lengthways if rectangular) and punch holes at even intervals along each side. Cut thin strips of crepe paper and thread through the holes, knotting at each end. Insert items that you wish to wrap and tie at the top with ribbon.

Bottles come in interesting shapes and colours. Dress-up a bottle of herb vinegar with a raffia bow tied around the neck or handle.

Old boxes can be re-used: paint them, cover with paper or festoon with ribbons. Take the bottom half of a flat box, punch holes through the corners and tie with bows to make a pretty presentation box for biscuits and slices.

Purchase patterned, papier-maché or glossy gift boxes and individualise them with some colourful fabric lining in interesting textures; trim with braid or ribbon.

Terracotta pots and trays, bowls and baskets make lovely containers for food. A fruit cake, biscuits or sweets will look great in a large pot wrapped in clear cellophane and finished with ribbon or coloured string. An inexpensive tea towel is a perfect wrapping for homemade muffins.

Create a seaside theme by wrapping boxes and jars in handmade paper or calico, then tying or knotting rope around them. Attach shells and other beach paraphernalia with glue and tape, or secure them beneath the rope.

To finish, raffia, rope and paper ribbon combine well with natural and brown papers, calico and muslin. Form wired ribbons in different widths, patterns and colours into cascading lengths or full bows. Preserved fruit slices, citrus peel strips, and fresh grapes or berries look great on top of jars, or use fresh or dried flowers. Attach cardboard or thick paper gift tags.

Use shells, flowers, leaves, fabric, cardboard, interesting bottles and jars, and a dash of imagination, to dress up your gifts.

Cakes, Slices & Biscuits

Traditional favourites or something a little different, home-baked goodies like these are sure to tempt them at the cake stall. Pack them in attractive boxes or colourful wrapping to make wonderful gifts.

Blueberry Muffins

Preparation time:
  20 minutes
Total cooking time:
  15–20 minutes
Makes 14

2 cups plain flour
2^1/2 teaspoons baking
  powder
^{1}/4 teaspoon
  bicarbonate of soda
pinch salt
^{2}/3 cup caster sugar
1–2 teaspoons grated
  lemon rind
1 cup fresh blueberries
1 egg
1 cup milk
90 g butter, melted

1. Preheat oven to moderate 180°C. Brush fourteen ^{1}/3-cup capacity muffin cups with oil or melted butter. Place combined sifted flour, baking powder, soda and salt into a large bowl. Add sugar and rind; mix well. Stir in blueberries.
2. Whisk together egg, milk and cooled melted butter in a large jug. Pour onto dry ingredients; using large metal spoon, mix together thoroughly but quickly until smooth.
3. Spoon into muffin cups until ^{2}/3 full. Bake for 15–20 minutes or until muffins have risen and are lightly browned, and until a skewer comes out clean when inserted in centre. Leave in tins for 3–5 minutes before placing on wire racks to cool.

HINT
If using frozen berries, add at the last minute, while still frozen. Fresh or frozen raspberries may also be used. Cooled muffins may be iced with a thin lemon icing.

Blueberry Muffins (top) and Family Chocolate Cake

Family Chocolate Cake

Preparation time:
  15 minutes
Total cooking time:
  50 minutes
Makes one 20 cm round cake

1¹/2 cups self-raising flour
¹/2 cup cocoa powder
1 cup caster sugar
200 g plain yoghurt
2 eggs
200 g butter, melted
50 g dark chocolate, grated

Icing
50 g dark chocolate, chopped
50 g butter
¹/2 cup icing sugar
1–2 tablespoons yoghurt or sour cream

1. Preheat oven to moderate 180°C. Brush a deep 20 cm tin with oil or melted butter; line base and sides with paper; grease paper.
2. Place flour, cocoa powder and sugar into food processor. Add yoghurt, eggs and butter. Using the pulse action, process for 15 seconds or until mixture is smooth. Add grated chocolate and process until ingredients are combined.
3. Pour mixture into prepared tin; smooth the surface. Bake for 50 minutes or until a skewer comes out clean when inserted into the centre of cake.
4. Stand cake in tin for 10 minutes before turning onto a wire rack to cool.
5. ***To make Icing:*** Place chocolate in small heatproof bowl. Stand bowl over a pan of barely simmering water and stir until chocolate has melted; remove from heat. Beat butter and icing sugar with electric beaters in small bowl until smooth and creamy. Add chocolate and yoghurt or sour cream; beat well until combined. Spread evenly over top of cake using a palette knife. Decorate top with whole, fresh strawberries, if desired.

> **HINT**
> Take care when melting chocolate to prevent any moisture coming into contact with the chocolate. If this happens the chocolate may become a rough, unworkable mass.

Chewy Muesli Bars

Preparation time:
  10 minutes
Total cooking time:
  45 minutes
Makes 24 bars

125 g unsalted butter
¹/2 cup caster sugar
¹/2 cup soft brown sugar, lightly packed
2 tablespoons honey
3¹/2 cups untoasted muesli
³/4 cup desiccated coconut
1 teaspoon ground cinnamon
¹/2 cup glacé cherries, chopped
¹/2 cup sultanas
¹/2 cup currants

1. Preheat oven to moderately slow 160°C. Brush a 30 x 20 cm rectangular tin with oil or melted butter. Line base and sides with paper; grease paper.
2. Combine butter, sugars and honey in a small pan. Stir over low heat until sugar has dissolved and butter has melted. Remove from heat.
3. Place muesli, coconut, cinnamon, cherries, sultanas, and currants in a large bowl; stir to combine. Make a well in centre. Pour butter mixture

Chewy Muesli Bars

onto dry ingredients; combine thoroughly.
4. Press the mixture firmly into prepared tin. Using a sharp knife, mark top of slice into 24 equal bars. Bake for 35 minutes, reduce oven temperature to very slow 120°C and cook for another 10 minutes. Leave slice in tin for 15 minutes before turning onto a board to cool. Cut into bars when completely cold. Store Muesli Bars in an airtight container in the refrigerator for up to one week.

Note: Pipe a pattern in melted chocolate to decorate, if desired.

Shortbread

Preparation time:
  20 minutes
Total cooking time:
  25 minutes + 30
  minutes refrigeration
*Makes 2 shortbread
rounds*

250 g butter, chopped
*1/2 teaspoon vanilla
  essence*
3/4 cup icing sugar
2 cups plain flour
1/2 cup rice flour

1. Preheat oven to
moderate 180°C. Line
two oven trays with
baking paper.
2. Using electric
beaters, beat butter and
essence in small bowl
until light and creamy.
Transfer to large bowl.
Add sifted icing sugar,
beat another minute.
3. Using a wooden
spoon, fold in sifted
flours a spoonful at a
time; mix well. Place
dough in refrigerator
for 30 minutes until
firm. Divide dough into
two portions. Flatten
slightly, then roll each
into a circle, between
two sheets of baking
paper, to a thickness of
5–6 mm. Carefully
transfer to trays.
4. Crimp circle edges
with fingers, or use a
fork. Prick all over with
a skewer. Score across
each circle to mark out

8 wedges. Bake 20–25
minutes, or until golden
and crisp. Cut into
wedges along score
lines. Transfer to wire
rack while still warm;
leave to cool.

Dark Ginger and Treacle Cake

Preparation time:
  30 minutes
Total cooking time:
  50–60 minutes
*Makes one 22 cm ring
cake*

*fine stale breadcrumbs
  or cornflake crumbs*
125 g butter, softened
*1/2 cup soft brown
  sugar*
1/3 cup black treacle
3 eggs
2 cups plain flour
1 teaspoon bicarbonate
  of soda
2 teaspoons ground
  cloves
1 teaspoon ground
  cinnamon
1 teaspoon ground
  ginger
2/3 cup sour cream
100 g preserved ginger,
  finely chopped and
  including syrup, or *1/2
  cup chunky ginger
  conserve*

Lemon Glaze
2/3 cup icing sugar
*1–2 tablespoons lemon
  juice*
50 g butter, softened

1. Preheat oven to
moderately slow
160°C. Brush a round
22 cm deep ring or
baba tin with oil or
melted butter; coat
inside of tin with bread
or cornflake crumbs.
2. Beat butter and
sugar with electric
beaters until light and
creamy. Beat in treacle.
3. Add eggs gradually,
beating well after each
addition. Using a large
metal spoon, fold in the
sifted flour, soda and
spices with sour cream.
Fold in chopped ginger
and syrup or conserve.
4. Spoon into prepared
tin; smooth the surface.
Bake 50–60 minutes, or
until a fine skewer
comes out clean when
inserted in centre.
Leave in tin 10 minutes
before turning onto a
wire rack to cool.
To make Lemon Glaze:
Combine icing sugar,
juice and butter in a
small heatproof bowl.
Stand bowl over a pan
of simmering water and
stir until smooth.
Remove from heat,
brush over warm cake.
Decorate with candied
orange peel and fresh
strawberries, if desired.

Dark Ginger & Treacle Cake (top) and Shortbread

Panforte

Preparation time:
  30 minutes
Total cooking time:
  30 minutes
*Makes two 22 cm
square or round cakes*

250 g almonds
250 g hazelnuts
750 g mixed dried
  fruits: seeded raisins,
  pitted prunes, pitted
  dates, soft dried figs,
  mixed peel
2 cups (250 g) plain
  flour
1 tablespoon mixed
  spice
1 tablespoon ground
  cinnamon
1¹/4 cups (300 g) caster
  sugar
1 cup honey
icing sugar, for dusting

1. Preheat oven to
moderate 180°C. Brush
two 22 cm shallow
round or square cake
tins with melted butter
or oil. Line base and
sides with baking paper.
2. Place almonds and
hazelnuts on an oven
tray. Roast in oven for
8–10 minutes, or until
hazelnut skins start to
peel. Remove from
oven. Lower oven heat
to moderately slow
160°C. Wrap hazelnuts
in a cloth and rub
vigorously to remove the
skins. Place whole nuts
in a large mixing bowl.

3. Chop the dried fruit
roughly and add to
bowl. Sift flour and
spices over fruit in bowl.
4. Place sugar and
honey in small pan. Stir
over low heat until
sugar has melted and
mixture is smooth. Bring
to boil, reduce heat and
simmer for about 10–15
minutes or until syrup
reaches 116°C–120°C
on a sugar thermometer
(immerse the bulb of the
thermometer in the
syrup after it has come
to the boil), or a
teaspoon of syrup forms
a soft ball when
dropped into a bowl of
iced water. Add syrup to
fruit and flour in bowl.
Using a large metal
spoon, stir until well
combined—mixture will
be stiff.
5. Spoon mixture
evenly into prepared
tins. Flatten with wet
hands—mixture should
be approximately 2 cm
deep. Bake 30 minutes.
Leave in tin on wire
rack to cool.
6. When cake is cool,
remove from tin; peel off
baking paper. Wrap in
plastic wrap and then in
foil. Refrigerate, or store
in a cool, dry place, until
needed. (Texture and
flavour of cake will
improve with keeping.)
Serve, dusted with icing
sugar, cut into very thin
slices or small squares.

Chocolate
Brownies

Preparation time:
  20 minutes
Total cooking time:
  35–40 minutes
Makes 16 squares

160 g dark chocolate,
  chopped
125 g butter
2 eggs, lightly beaten
³/4 cup caster sugar
1 teaspoon vanilla
  essence
1 cup plain flour
³/4 cup chopped
  walnuts or pecans

1. Preheat oven to
moderate 180°C. Brush
20 cm square cake tin
with oil or melted butter;
line base with baking
paper. Place chocolate
and butter in a medium
heatproof bowl over
simmering water. Stir
until melted and smooth.
Remove from heat, cool.
2. Stir in eggs, sugar and
essence. Add sifted flour
and nuts, combine well
(do not over-beat).
3. Pour mixture into tin.
Bake for 20–25 minutes
or until skewer comes
out clean when inserted
in centre. Cool in tin; cut
into squares. Dust with a
little combined cocoa
and icing sugar and top
with pecans, if desired.

Chocolate Brownies (top) and Panforte

Lemon Curd Tartlets

Preparation time:
40 minutes +
standing
Total cooking time:
15 minutes
Makes 18

1 cup plain flour
60 g chilled butter,
chopped
2 egg yolks
1/4 cup caster sugar
1–2 teaspoons grated
lemon rind
1 tablespoon lemon
juice

Filling
1/2 cup caster sugar
2/3 cup fresh lemon
juice, strained
2 tablespoons thick
cream or 60 g butter,
extra
3 eggs
2 egg yolks, extra

1. Place flour in food
processor. Add butter,
process 15–20 seconds
until mixture resembles
fine breadcrumbs. Add
yolks, sugar, rind and
juice. Process for
20–30 seconds until
mixture just comes
together. Turn onto a
floured surface and
knead gently into a
ball. Wrap in plastic
wrap and refrigerate
for 45–60 minutes.
2. Roll pastry out

thinly on a lightly
floured surface, or
between two sheets of
baking paper. Cut into
circles using a round
6–7 cm cutter. Brush
pastry rounds with a
little oil or melted
butter and press rounds
gently into shallow
patty tins; prick all over
with a fine skewer or
fork. Place in freezer
for 30 minutes or
longer before baking.
3. Preheat oven to
moderate 180°C. Cut
sheets of baking paper
large enough to cover
each pastry circle.
Spread a layer of dried
beans or rice evenly
over paper. Bake for
10 minutes, or until
golden and crisp.
Remove paper and
beans or rice.
4. **To make Filling:**
Whisk sugar with
lemon juice in a
medium bowl. Whisk
in cream or butter, eggs
and yolks. Mix well.
Transfer mixture to
medium pan. Whisk
over medium heat for
4 minutes, or until the
mixture is thickened
and smooth. Spoon
evenly into pastry
shells, leaving a small
edge of pastry. Bake
tartlets for another
8–10 minutes. Cool,
then transfer to a wire
rack. Decorate tartlets
with whipped cream
and candied peel, if
desired.

Fig and Nut Roll

Preparation time:
20 minutes
Total cooking time:
40 minutes
Makes 1 large or 2
small rolls

1 cup soft pitted dried
figs, or dried dates,
chopped
3/4 cup soft brown
sugar
1 teaspoon bicarbonate
of soda
60 g butter, chopped
1–2 teaspoons grated
orange rind
1 cup boiling water
2 cups (250 g)
self-raising flour
1/4 teaspoon ground
nutmeg
1/4 teaspoon ground
cinnamon
1/4 teaspoon ground
allspice
1/4 teaspoon ground
ginger
1 egg
1 teaspoon vanilla
essence
1 cup (125 g) pecans,
toasted and chopped

1. Place figs or dates,
sugar, soda, butter and
rind in a large bowl.
Pour boiling water
over. Stir together until
butter and sugar are
melted. Allow to cool.
2. Preheat oven to
moderate 180°C. Brush
base and sides of a
5-cup roll tin, or two

Lemon Curd Tartlets (top) and Fig and Nut Roll.

170 mm x 80 mm roll tins, with melted butter. Leave a 5 cm collar of baking paper above edge of tin.

3. Sift flour and spices together. In a small bowl, whisk egg with essence. Using a large metal spoon, fold flour and pecans alternately with egg into cooled cake mixture. Stir until smooth.

4. Spoon batter into roll tin(s). Bake with tins upright on an oven tray in centre of oven for 35–40 minutes or until a skewer comes out clean when inserted in centre; the top should spring back when pressed with a finger. Cool in tin 5 minutes before turning onto wire rack to cool. Serve roll sliced, spread with butter.

Note: Cool completely before slicing to prevent crumbling.

Dark Carrot Cake with Rich Cream Cheese Frosting

Preparation time:
  30 minutes
Total cooking time:
  1 hour 20 minutes
Makes one 24 cm round cake

2 cups self-raising flour
2 teaspoons ground
  cinnamon
1 teaspoon ground
  cloves
1 teaspoon ground
  ginger
2 teaspoons
  bicarbonate of soda
1 cup oil
1 cup soft brown sugar
4 eggs
1/2 cup golden syrup
350 g grated carrot

Cream Cheese Frosting
250 g cream cheese
60 g butter, softened
1 cup icing sugar
1 teaspoon vanilla
  essence or lemon juice
1 teaspoon grated
  lemon rind

1. Preheat oven to moderate 180°C. Brush a 24 cm deep, round springform cake tin with melted butter; line base and sides with baking paper. Sift together flour, spices and soda.
2. Place oil, sugar, eggs and golden syrup in food processor. Add flour and spices and process 20–30 seconds. Add carrot and process again until well combined. Pour the mixture into prepared tin; smooth surface. Bake for 30 minutes. Reduce heat to moderately slow 160°C and cook for another 40–50 minutes, or until a skewer comes out clean when inserted in centre of cake. Leave the cake in the tin for 10 minutes before turning onto a wire rack to cool.
3. When cake is cool, cut horizontally into two layers. Place base layer on a board or plate and spread with half the Cream Cheese Frosting. Replace top layer and spread remaining frosting over top of cake. Decorate cake with carrot curls and chopped walnuts, if desired. For best results, serve cake the next day.
4. ***To make Cream Cheese Frosting:*** Beat cream cheese with electric beaters in a medium bowl until smooth. Add butter, icing sugar, essence or juice, and rind; beat together until mixture is light and creamy.

Traditional Coconut Macaroons

Preparation time:
  20 minutes
Total cooking time:
  20 minutes
Makes 25

2 egg whites
3/4 cup caster sugar
1 1/2 cups desiccated
  coconut
200 g dark chocolate,
  melted

1. Preheat oven to slow 150°C. Line two oven trays with baking paper. Beat egg whites in small bowl until firm peaks form. Add sugar gradually, beating well after each addition and until sugar has dissolved and mixture is thick and glossy.
2. Transfer to large bowl, add coconut. Using a large metal spoon, fold gently until ingredients are just combined. Drop level tablespoons of mixture onto trays, about 3 cm apart. Bake 20 minutes or until lightly golden.
3. Cool completely on wire rack. Dip bases in melted chocolate and allow to set.

---

*Dark Carrot Cake with Rich Cream Cheese
Frosting (top) and Traditional
Coconut Macaroons*

Citrus Dried Fruit Delights

Preparation time:
  15 minutes
Total cooking time:
  20 minutes
Makes 18 pieces

1 cup self-raising flour
1 teaspoon cinnamon
3/4 cup caster sugar
1/2 cup sultanas
1/4 cup dried apricots, chopped
1/4 cup dried pears, chopped
1/4 cup dried apples, chopped
2 eggs, lightly beaten
90 g butter, melted

Lemon Glacé Icing
1 cup icing sugar
15 g unsalted butter, melted
3–4 teaspoons lemon juice

1. Preheat oven to moderate 180°C. Brush a 20 cm square cake tin with oil or melted butter. Line base with baking paper; grease the paper.
2. Sift flour, cinnamon and sugar into a large bowl. Add sultanas and dried fruit, stir. Make a well in the centre.
3. Add combined eggs and butter. Using a wooden spoon, mix well until smooth; do not over-beat. Pour into

prepared tin, smooth surface. Bake for 20 minutes or until a skewer comes out clean when inserted in the centre. Leave cake in tin for 5 minutes before turning onto a wire rack to cool.
4. Cut into bars and spread with Lemon Glacé Icing. Decorate with chopped dried apricot, if desired.
5. *To Make Lemon Glacé Icing:* In a small bowl, combine sifted icing sugar, melted butter, and enough lemon juice to form a firm paste. Stand bowl over pan of simmering water, stirring until icing is smooth and glossy—do not over-beat or icing will become dull and grainy. Remove from heat; spread over each piece of Fruit Delight, using a flat-bladed knife.

Note: Citrus Dried Fruit Delights can be stored in an airtight container for up to five days. They will keep, un-iced, in the freezer for up to three months.

Rich Prune and Apricot Cakes

Preparation time:
  30 minutes
Total cooking time:
  50-60 minutes
Makes two bar cakes

1/2 cup currants
250 g pitted prunes, chopped
100 g dried apricots, halved
1/3 cup fruit mince
1/2 cup mixed dried fruits
1/4 cup brandy
150 g butter
1/4 cup soft brown sugar
1/4 cup treacle
2 tablespoons malt extract
2 eggs
1/3 cup self raising flour
2/3 cup plain flour
1/4 teaspoon bicarbonate of soda
1 teaspoon mixed spice

1. Preheat oven to slow 150°C. Brush two 26 x 8 x 5 cm bar tins with oil or melted butter. Line base and sides with paper, extending paper 1–2 cm above edge of tin on all sides. Combine currants, prunes, apricots, fruit mince, mixed fruits and brandy in medium pan. Stir over medium heat until all brandy has been absorbed. Remove from heat, cool slightly.

Rich Prune and Apricot Cakes (top) and Citrus Dried Fruit Delights

2. Beat butter and sugar with electric beaters in small mixing bowl until light and creamy. Add treacle and malt and beat until ingredients are well combined. Add eggs gradually, beating well after each addition. Transfer to a large mixing bowl. Using a metal spoon, gradually fold in the sifted flours, soda and spice. Stir until smooth. Add the fruit mixture and stir until well combined.

3. Spoon mixture evenly into tins; smooth the surface. Tap the tins gently on bench to remove excess air bubbles from the mixture. Stand the tins on a baking tray and bake for 50–55 minutes or until a skewer comes out clean when inserted into the centre of the cakes. Leave cakes in the tins for 30 minutes before turning them onto a wire rack to cool. When the cakes are cool, dust the tops with sifted icing sugar.

17

Choc-chip Peanut Cookies

Preparation time:
  15 minutes
Total cooking time:
  20 minutes
Makes 30

125 g butter
1/2 cup sugar
1/4 cup soft brown
  sugar, firmly packed
1 egg
1 cup self-raising flour
1/2 cup plain flour
3/4 cup unsalted roasted
  peanuts
3/4 cup dark choc dots

1. Preheat oven to moderate 180°C. Line two 32 x 28 cm biscuit trays with baking paper. Using electric beaters, beat butter and sugars until light and fluffy. Add the egg and beat thoroughly.
2. Transfer to a large mixing bowl; add sifted flours, peanuts, and choc dots. Using a large metal spoon, stir until ingredients are just combined and the mixture is smooth.
3. Knead the mixture lightly to form a soft dough. Roll one level tablespoon at a time into a ball.
4. Arrange on trays, allowing room for spreading. Flatten gently with fingers.

Bake for 15–20 minutes, or until golden. Remove biscuits from oven, cool on trays for 5 minutes before transferring to wire rack to cool completely.

Jam and Cream Sponge Cake

Preparation time:
  20 minutes
Total cooking time:
  25 minutes
Makes one 20 cm cake

3 eggs
1/3 cup (80 g) caster
  sugar
1 teaspoon vanilla
  essence
1–2 teaspoons grated
  lemon or orange rind
1/2 cup (80 g) self-
  raising flour, sifted
45 g butter, melted
1 1/4 cups thick or
  pouring cream
1–2 tablespoons icing
  sugar
1/3 cup strawberry or
  raspberry jam or
  lemon butter
sifted icing sugar

1. Preheat oven to moderate 180°C. Brush two 17 cm shallow round cake tins with oil or melted butter; line base with baking paper.

Dust base and sides of tin with flour; shake out excess.
2. Place eggs and sugar into large heatproof bowl. Stand bowl over a pan of simmering water. Using hand-held electric beater or wire whisk, whisk until thick and pale yellow in colour. Remove bowl from heat. Add essence and rind and beat for another 7–10 minutes, until lifted beater leaves a ribbon on the surface. Using a metal spoon, lightly fold in flour, incorporating as much air as possible. Fold in melted butter (mixture will deflate). Pour batter evenly into prepared tins, gently smooth surface.
3. Bake 20–25 minutes or until the top of the cake springs back when pressed with finger. Allow to cool in tin for 5 minutes before turning onto wire rack to cool completely.
4. Beat cream and icing sugar until mixture holds firm peaks. Place one cake on board or plate. Spread with jam or lemon butter and then cream. Top with remaining cake. Dust top with sifted icing sugar and decorate sponge with a strawberry, if desired.

Jam and Cream Sponge Cake (top)
and Choc-chip Peanut Cookies

Anzac Biscuits

Preparation time:
15 minutes
Total cooking time:
20 minutes
Makes 28

1 cup plain flour
3/4 cup sugar
1 cup rolled oats
3/4 cup desiccated
  coconut
125 g unsalted butter
2 tablespoons golden
  syrup
1/2 teaspoon
  bicarbonate of soda
1 tablespoon boiling
  water

1. Preheat oven to
moderate 180°C. Line
two 32 x 28 cm biscuit
trays with baking
paper. Sift flour into a
large mixing bowl. Add
sugar, oats, and
coconut; make a well in
the centre.
2. Combine butter and
golden syrup in small
pan. Stir over low heat
until butter has melted
and mixture is smooth;
remove from heat.
Dissolve soda in water;
add immediately to
butter mixture—it will
foam up instantly. Add
butter mixture to dry
ingredients. Using a
wooden spoon, stir well
until combined.
3. Shape one level
tablespoon of mixture
at a time into a ball,
place on prepared tray.
Flatten gently with
fingers, allowing room
for spreading. Bake for
15–20 minutes, or until
just brown.
4. Remove biscuits
from oven and transfer
to a wire rack to cool.

Strawberry Coconut Slice

Preparation time:
30 minutes
Total cooking time:
40 minutes
Makes 18 pieces

125 g butter
1/4 cup custard powder
3/4 cup plain flour
1/3 cup sugar
1 egg, lightly beaten
3/4 cup strawberry jam

Topping
2 eggs, separated
1/3 cup caster sugar
1 teaspoon vanilla
  essence
3 cups desiccated
  coconut

1. Preheat oven to
moderate 180°C. Brush
the base and sides of a
20 x 30 cm shallow
oblong tin with melted
butter or oil. Line base
with baking paper.
2. Place butter, custard
powder, flour and sugar
in a medium mixing
bowl. Rub butter into
dry ingredients until it
resembles coarse
breadcrumbs. Add egg
and mix to form a
smooth paste.
3. Spread mixture
evenly over base of
prepared tin. Bake in
preheated oven for
20 minutes, or until
firm and golden. Cool.
Spread base with
warmed jam.
4. ***To make Topping:***
Using electric beaters,
beat egg whites in a
small bowl until stiff
peaks form. Add sugar
gradually, beating well
after each addition.
Transfer mixture to
large bowl. Add egg
yolks and essence. Add
coconut and stir
through gently and
lightly. Spread topping
over slice. Bake for
another 15–20 minutes
or until golden. Allow
slice to cool completely
before cutting into
squares with a
long-bladed, sharp
knife. Slice will keep
for up to three days in
an airtight container.

Note: Slice may be
made using jams such
as apricot, blackberry
or raspberry.

Anzac Biscuits (top) and Strawberry Coconut Slice

Honey Nut Joys

Preparation time:
  30 minutes
Total cooking time:
  15 minutes
Makes 24 biscuits

4 cups cornflakes
100 g butter
¹/4 cup caster sugar
2 tablespoons honey
¹/2 cup crushed nuts
2 tablespoons sesame
  seeds, toasted

1. Preheat oven to moderate 180°C. Line two 12-cup deep patty tins with patty cases.
2. Place the cornflakes in a large bowl. Combine the butter, sugar and honey in a small pan. Stir over medium heat without boiling until the sugar has dissolved. Bring to the boil, then remove from heat.
3. Pour the mixture over the cornflakes; add the crushed nuts and sesame seeds. Stir quickly until all ingredients are well combined and cornflakes are coated with syrup.
4. Place spoonfuls of the cornflake mixture evenly into the prepared tins. Bake for 10 minutes, or until Honey Nut Joys are just golden and slightly crisp. Leave to stand for 10 minutes in tins before transferring to a wire rack to cool.

Note: Store in an airtight container in a cool, dry place for up to a week.

Caramel Slice

Preparation time:
  15 minutes
Total cooking time:
  30 minutes
Makes 30

³/4 cup desiccated
  coconut
¹/3 cup soft brown
  sugar
³/4 cup self-raising flour
100 g butter, melted
1 teaspoon vanilla
  essence

Topping
400 g sweetened
  condensed milk
30 g butter
2 tablespoons golden
  syrup
2 teaspoons instant
  coffee
2 teaspoons hot water

Icing
120 g dark chocolate,
  chopped
60 g butter, chopped

1. Preheat oven to 180°C. Line base and sides of deep 28 x 18 cm rectangular tin with baking paper, extending over all sides of the tin.
2. Place the coconut, sugar and flour in a large bowl and mix together. Make a well in the centre. Stir in melted butter and essence; mix well. Press mixture evenly into base of prepared tin. Bake 12–15 minutes; remove slice from the oven before the edges begin to brown.
3. *To make Topping:* Place condensed milk, butter, golden syrup, and combined coffee and water in a small pan. Stir over medium heat until mixture boils. Reduce heat and simmer, stirring, for another 5 minutes. Pour caramel mixture over cooked slice base. Return tray to oven and bake slice for another 10 minutes. Remove from oven and set aside to cool in tin.
4. *To make Icing:* Place the chocolate and butter in a small, heatproof bowl. Stand the bowl over a pan of simmering water. Stir until chocolate and butter have melted and the mixture is smooth. Spread icing evenly over the still-warm caramel layer of slice;

Caramel Slice (top) and Honey Nut Joys

smooth icing using a flat-bladed knife. Refrigerate Caramel Slice until icing sets.

Cut into squares or bars. Lift carefully from tin, removing corner slice first.

Note: Store Caramel Slice in an airtight container in a cool place for up to a week.

Jams, Preserves & Condiments

There is something luxurious about these hand-made gourmet delights in bottles and jars. Whether you make them as gifts or for the fete, they will be so much more appreciated than their commercial equivalents.

Cumquats in Liqueur

Preparation time:
  15 minutes
Total cooking time:
  50 minutes
Makes about 3 cups

500 g cumquats
1 cup sugar
$3/4$ cup water
$1/4$ cup orange-
  flavoured liqueur

1. Cut a cross in top of each cumquat; pack into heatproof, sterilised jars.
2. Combine sugar and water in small heavy-based pan. Bring to boil, then boil for 1 minute. Stir in liqueur.
3. Pour syrup over cumquats, leaving 1 cm at the top of jars. Screw lids on loosely—do not fully tighten.
4. Place layers of newspaper on bottom of a large, heavy-based pan. Place jars on top and cover with enough hot water to reach top of jar rims.
5. Bring water slowly to simmer. Reduce heat slightly then simmer jars for 20 minutes, or until the cumquats start to look clear.
6. Remove jars carefully. Immediately tighten lids fully and cool completely. Label and date jars. Store in a cool, dark place for 2 months, turning jars upside-down every couple of weeks.

HINT
Cumquats will develop more flavour the longer they are left to mature. Serve with a spoonful of syrup.

Chilli Oil (left) and Cumquats in Liqueur

Chilli Oil

Preparation time:
  10 minutes
Total cooking time:
  5 minutes +
  2 days standing
Makes 2 1/2 cups

2 1/2 cups vegetable oil
3 fresh whole chillies
1 cinnamon stick
2 teaspoons black
  peppercorns
fresh, whole pieces of
  chosen flavourings—
  herbs or whole spices

1. Heat the oil in a large heavy-based pan. Add the chillies, cinnamon stick and peppercorns. Remove from heat then cover and leave to stand for 2–3 days.
2. Strain the oil into a sterilised bottle. Add fresh, whole flavourings to bottle.
3. Seal and label. Store in a cool, dark place.

> **HINT**
> Fresh herbs such as rosemary, basil, sage or lemon grass may be substituted for the chillies.

Lemon Butter

Preparation time:
  10 minutes
Total cooking time:
  20 minutes
Makes about 2 cups

4 eggs, lightly beaten
3/4 cup sugar
1/2 cup lemon juice
2 teaspoons finely
  grated lemon rind
125 g unsalted butter,
  chopped

1. Place eggs and sugar in a large heatproof bowl. Place bowl over a pan of simmering water and stir constantly with a wire whisk until sugar has dissolved.
2. Add the lemon juice, grated rind and butter; whisk until mixture is smooth and butter has melted. Beat constantly with a wooden spoon over barely simmering water for about 20 minutes, or until the mixture thickens and coats the back of a spoon. Remove from heat immediately. (Do not allow mixture to boil or it will curdle.)
3. Pour or ladle warm lemon butter into hot, sterilised jars and seal immediately. Allow to cool completely before labelling and storing in a cool, dark place.

Easy Strawberry Jam

Preparation time:
  10 minutes +
  standing
Total cooking time:
  20 minutes
Makes 2 cups

2 punnets ripe
  strawberries (500 g),
  washed and hulled
2. cups sugar
2 tablespoons lemon
  juice

1. Combine the strawberries and sugar in a medium heavy-based pan. Allow to stand for 10 minutes.
2. Add lemon juice to the pan. Stir gently over low to medium heat, without boiling, until sugar has completely dissolved. Bring slowly to the boil, reduce heat and simmer on low to medium heat for 35 minutes, or until jam gels when tested.
3. Remove jam from heat and allow bubbles to subside. Set aside for 2 minutes. Ladle the hot mixture into hot, sterilised jars and seal immediately. Label and date jars when cool. Store in a cool, dark place. Refrigerate jam after opening.

Lemon Butter and Easy Strawberry Jam

Rich Mint Jelly

Preparation time:
  20 minutes +
  overnight standing
Total cooking time:
  40 minutes
Makes about 3¹/₂ cups

1 kg green apples
1 litre water
¹/₂ cup lemon juice
2¹/₂ cups mint leaves
sugar
¹/₂ cup extra mint
  leaves, finely chopped
2–3 drops green food
  colouring

1. Wash and cut apples into thick slices but do not peel or core.
2. Combine apple, water, juice and mint leaves in a large heavy-based pan; bring to boil. Reduce heat slightly and cook, uncovered, sfor 10–15 minutes or until apple forms a soft pulp.

Break up any large pieces with a wooden spoon.
3. Strain mixture through muslin into a bowl—do not press liquid through muslin or it will become cloudy. Leave overnight. Measure the strained juice and return it to pan. Add 1 cup of sugar for each cup of liquid. Stir over low heat without boiling until sugar has dissolved completely. Bring to boil, reduce heat slightly; boil on low heat for about 20 minutes, or until mixture gels when tested.
4. Add extra mint and colouring, stir well until no streaking is visible and mint is distributed evenly. Remove from heat, set aside 5 minutes. Pour into hot, sterilised jars, seal immediately. Label and date the jars when cool. Store mint jelly in a cool, dark place for up to 12 months.

Rich Mint Jelly

1. Cut the washed apples into thick slices; do not peel or core.

2. Break up any large pieces of cooked apple with a wooden spoon.

3. Strain the mixture through a piece of muslin into a bowl.

4. Add extra mint and green food colouring to mixture, stirring well.

Fig and Spice Jam

Preparation time:
  10 minutes +
  overnight standing
Total cooking time:
  35 minutes
Makes 1 litre

500 g dried dessert figs
1 litre water
1/3 cup lemon juice
3 cups sugar, warmed
1/4 cup glacé ginger,
  chopped
2 teaspoons finely
  grated lemon rind
1 teaspoon whole
  cloves

1. Chop figs finely and place in medium bowl. Cover with the water and leave overnight.
2. The next day, transfer the figs and water to a large heavy-based pan. Bring to the boil, then reduce heat, cover and simmer for 10–15 minutes or until the figs become tender and plump.
3. Add the lemon juice, sugar, ginger, rind and cloves. Stir constantly over low heat until sugar has completely dissolved. Bring to the boil, reduce heat slightly and boil for 15–20 minutes, or until the mixture gels when tested; stir occasionally with a wooden spoon. Stir the mixture more frequently towards the end of cooking to make sure it does not catch or burn.
4. Remove jam from heat and set aside for 2 minutes. Using a heatproof jug, pour the jam into hot, sterilised jars and seal them immediately. Label and date the jars when cool.

Note: Fig and Spice Jam will keep in a cool, dark place for up to 12 months.

Pears in Rum

Preparation time:
  20 minutes
Total cooking time:
  20 minutes
Makes about 8 halves

500 g small corella or
  paradise pears
1*1/2 cups sugar*
1 cup water
2 cinnamon sticks
1/4 cup dark rum

1. Wash the pears, then peel and core (if using paradise pears, peel and leave whole). Place in a large bowl and cover with water. Set aside.
2. Place sugar and water in a medium heavy-based pan. Stir over low heat, without boiling, until sugar has completely dissolved. Brush sugar crystals from sides of pan with a wet pastry brush. Bring to boil, reduce heat slightly and boil syrup for 10 minutes without stirring.
3. Drain water from pears. Place pears and cinnamon sticks into a pan with syrup and simmer for another 5–6 minutes, or until the pears are tender. Carefully turn the fruit several times during cooking to coat with syrup. Remove pears from syrup and pack into sterilised jars.
4. Add rum to the syrup and return to heat. Bring to boil and boil for 2–3 minutes. Gently pour the syrup over the fruit in jars and seal. Set aside for 2–3 days, to allow flavour to penetrate fruit, before serving.

HINT
Pears in Rum make a delicious summer dessert, served with ice-cream. In winter they can be heated and served with a generous dollop of thick cream, or with a creamy custard.

Pears in Rum (top) and Fig and Spice Jam

Dried Fruit Chutney

Preparation time:
15 minutes
Total cooking time:
35 minutes
Makes 3 cups

3 large green apples
$^1/_2$ cup pitted prunes, chopped
$^1/_2$ cup dates, chopped
$^1/_2$ cup dried apricots, chopped
$^1/_4$ cup lemon juice
$^3/_4$ cup sugar
1 cup white vinegar
$^1/_2$ cup water
$^1/_2$ teaspoon nutmeg

1. Peel, core and chop apples. Place all ingredients in a medium, heavy-based pan. Stir over medium heat until sugar has dissolved.
2. Increase heat to high and bring mixture to the boil. Reduce heat slightly and boil for 30–35 minutes, or until the chutney has thickened. Stir the mixture occasionally.
3. Remove chutney from heat and set aside for 5 minutes. Using a heatproof jug, pour mixture into hot, sterilised jars. Seal immediately. When cool, label and date jars. Store in a cool, dark place for up to 12 months.

Prunes in Rum

Preparation time:
10 minutes + 1 week standing
Total cooking time:
5 minutes
Makes 4 cups

750 g pitted prunes
$^3/_4$ cup dark rum
$^1/_4$ cup soft brown sugar, lightly packed
2 cinnamon sticks
rind of 1 lemon, cut into thick strips
2 cups water
3 whole cloves

1. Place prunes in a medium bowl. Place remaining ingredients in pan. Bring to boil. Remove from heat.
2. Pour syrup over prunes. Allow to cool completely and place in warm, sterilised jars, covering prunes completely with syrup. Seal jars, label and date.
3. Store in a cool dark place for 1 week before using. Refrigerate after opening—will keep for up to 12 months.

Herb Vinegar

Preparation time:
10 minutes
Total cooking time:
5 minutes +
2 days standing
Makes 2$^1/_2$ cups

1 lemon
2$^1/_2$ cups white vinegar
2 bay leaves
1 piece rosemary
2 tablespoons fresh oregano, chopped
sprigs of fresh herbs or fresh whole spices, for flavouring

1. Peel lemon, using a vegetable peeler, into thick strips. Remove any white pith with a sharp knife. Heat the vinegar in a small pan until simmering. Remove from heat, add flavourings.
2. Cover and allow to stand for 2 days, stirring occasionally.
3. Strain vinegar into a sterilised bottle. Add fresh flavourings.
4. Seal tightly. Label bottle and store in a cool place. Herb Vinegar will keep well for up to six months.

Note: This vinegar has a rich herb and citrus flavour and is ideal for dressing salads.

Clockwise from top left: Herb Vinegar, Dried Fruit Chutney and Prunes in Rum

Citrus Trio Marmalade

Preparation time:
  40 minutes + 20
  minutes standing
Total cooking time:
  1 hour 10 minutes
Makes 4 cups

2 grapefruit
3 limes
2 oranges
4¹/2 cups water
3³/4 cups sugar,
  warmed

1. Peel long strips of rind from grapefruit, limes and oranges, using a vegetable peeler; remove and retain any thick white pith. Slice rind into thin strips, using a sharp knife.
2. Squeeze juice from fruit, reserve juice. Place the seeds, pith, and flesh onto a piece of muslin and tie muslin with string.
3. Place the peel, juice, water and muslin bag in a large heavy-based pan. Bring to the boil, reduce heat and simmer, uncovered, for 45–50 minutes, or until contents of pan have reduced by half. Remove muslin bag, squeezing out excess juices. Add sugar to pan, stir until sugar has dissolved. Bring to the boil; boil steadily, uncovered, on low heat 15–20 minutes, or until a spoonful of mixture placed on a cold plate wrinkles when pushed with a finger.
4. Allow marmalade to stand 20 minutes. Skim gently if necessary. Pour into hot, sterilised jars; seal immediately. Label and date when cool.

Note: Blood oranges are delicious in this recipe.

Citrus Trio Marmalade

1. Remove and reserve thick white pith from grapefruit, lime and orange rind.

2. Place the muslin bag containing seeds, pith and flesh into the pan.

3. *Place a spoonful of mixture on a cold plate and push with your finger to test.*

4. *Leave marmalade to stand for 20 minutes, skimming gently if necessary.*

Whisky Mincemeat (Fruitmince)

Preparation time:
  20 minutes +
  overnight standing
  + 2 weeks standing
Total cooking time:
  Nil
Makes 4 cups

1 large green apple,
  peeled and grated
1 cup sultanas
1 cup raisins, finely
  chopped
1 cup currants
1/2 cup mixed peel
2 tablespoons glacé
  ginger, finely chopped
rind and juice of 1
  lemon
rind and juice of 1
  orange
1/3 cup blanched
  almonds, chopped
2 teaspoons mixed
  spice
1/2 cup soft brown
  sugar, lightly packed
1/4 cup whisky
50 g butter, melted

1. Place all ingredients
in a large, non-metal
mixing bowl. Stir until
thoroughly combined.
Cover, leave overnight.
2. Spoon into warm,
sterilised jars, seal at
once, label and date.
Leave 1–2 weeks before
using. Store mincemeat
in a cool, dark place for
up to 12 months.

HINT
Use mincemeat as a
filling for fruit tarts,
or decorate jars
with pretty ribbon
and fabric to make
Christmas gifts.

Mustard Pickles

Preparation time:
  15 minutes +
  overnight standing
Total cooking time:
  10–12 minutes
Makes about 4 cups

3 medium Lebanese
  cucumbers, chopped
1 large onion,
  chopped
200 g cauliflower, cut
  into tiny florets
1 large green capsicum,
  chopped
2 tablespoons salt
2 teaspoons brown
  mustard seeds
2 tablespoons mustard
  powder
1/2 teaspoon turmeric
  powder
1 bay leaf
1 cup malt vinegar
1/4 cup sugar
1 tablespoon cornflour
2 tablespoons water

---

1. Combine the
cucumbers, onion,
cauliflower, and
capsicum in a large
non-metal bowl.
Sprinkle vegetables
with salt and leave to
stand overnight.
2. Wash and drain the
vegetables, rinsing
thoroughly to remove
all salt. Place in a large
heavy-based pan. Add
the mustard seeds,
mustard powder,
turmeric, bay leaf,
vinegar and sugar. Stir
over low heat until
mixture boils. Simmer,
uncovered, for
8–10 minutes, or until
vegetables are tender.
3. Combine the
cornflour and water in
a small mixing bowl.
Add mixture to the pan
and stir through the
vegetables quickly.
Bring to the boil, then
remove from heat once
the mixture has
thickened.
4. Spoon pickles into
hot, sterilised jars and
seal immediately. When
the jars have cooled,
label and date.

Note: Most types of
pickling vegetables are
suitable for use in this
recipe. The selection
above will give a good
combination of
flavours and textures,
but experiment with
others if you prefer.

Mustard Pickles (top) and Whisky Mincemeat

WHISKEY
MINCE MEAT

Green Tomato Chutney

Preparation time:
  20 minutes
Total cooking time:
  1–1 1/2 hours
Makes about 5 cups

1.5 kg green tomatoes,
  chopped
2 small green apples,
  peeled and chopped
1 large onion, chopped
1 teaspoon salt
1/2 cup sultanas
1 teaspoon whole black
  peppercorns
1 tablespoon brown
  mustard seeds
2 cups soft brown
  sugar, lightly packed
2 cups white vinegar
1/2 teaspoon sweet
  paprika

1. Place all ingredients
in a large, heavy-based
pan. Stir over low heat
until sugar has
dissolved.
2. Increase heat to
medium and bring
mixture to the boil.
Simmer, uncovered, for
1–1 1/2 hours, or until
chutney has thickened.
Stir mixture
occasionally. Stir more
frequently towards the
end of cooking time to
ensure mixture does
not catch or burn.

3. Remove from heat,
set aside for 5 minutes.
Pour mixture into hot,
sterilised jars; seal
immediately. Label and
date when cool. Store
in a cool, dark place for
up to 12 months.

Note: Cooking time
will vary depending on
ripeness of tomatoes.

Sweet Rich Chilli Sauce

Preparation time:
  20 minutes
Total cooking time:
  35 minutes
Makes 3 cups

8–10 ripe egg or plum
  tomatoes, chopped
2 large green apples,
  chopped
1/2 cup dates,
  chopped
1/2 cup raisins
1/2 cup sultanas
1 cup white vinegar
1 teaspoon ground
  cinnamon
1 teaspoon ground
  paprika
2–3 fresh chillies,
  chopped
1/2 cup soft brown
  sugar, lightly packed

1. Combine all the
ingredients except the
sugar in a medium
heavy-based pan. Stir
until all ingredients are
thoroughly combined.
Bring to the boil,
reduce heat slightly and
boil for 20 minutes, or
until mixture is thick
and pulpy.
2. Remove sauce from
heat. Push the mixture
through a sieve and
return to the pan. Add
sugar and stir over
medium heat until it
has dissolved. Return
to boil and simmer for
another 10–15 minutes
or until the sauce has
thickened.
3. Use a heatproof jug
to pour the sauce into
hot, sterilised jars or
bottles. Seal at once
and leave to cool. Label
and date the bottles.

Note: Sweet Rich Chilli
Sauce may be bottled
without sieving if a
thicker, chunkier
version is preferred.

> **HINT**
> This sauce is
> delicious served
> either hot or cold.
> The amount of chilli
> can be varied
> according to taste.
> The recipe above is
> for a very mild
> sauce; for a hotter
> version, increase the
> number of chillies.

*Green Tomato Chutney (top) and
Sweet Rich Chilli Sauce*

Quick and Easy Plum Sauce

Preparation time:
  15 minutes
Total cooking time:
  35 minutes
Makes about 1 1/2 cups

1 teaspoon whole
  cloves
1 cinnamon stick
1 bay leaf
1 teaspoon whole black
  peppercorns
1 teaspoon brown
  mustard seeds
825 g can dark plums,
  drained and chopped
1 medium onion, finely
  chopped
1/2 cup soft brown
  sugar, lightly packed
1 1/2 cup malt vinegar

1. Place cloves,
cinnamon stick, bay
leaf, peppercorns and
mustard seeds on a
small, square piece of
muslin. Secure with a
piece of string.
2. Place plums, onion,
sugar and vinegar in a
large, heavy-based pan.
Stir over low heat until
sugar has dissolved.
3. Place muslin bag in
pan. Increase heat to
medium and bring to
the boil; reduce heat
slightly and boil for
30–35 minutes or until
sauce has thickened.
4. Remove from heat
and cool slightly. Place

mixture in food
processor and press the
pulse button for
20 seconds, or until
sauce is smooth and
free of large chunks.
5. Pour sauce into hot
sterilised bottles or jars
and seal immediately.
Label and date when
cool. Store in the
refrigerator for up to
six months.

Apricot and Ginger Jam

Preparation time:
  15 minutes +
  overnight standing
Total cooking time:
  1 hour
Makes 4 cups

500 g dried apricots
5 cups water
200 g preserved ginger
  in syrup, thinly sliced
3 3/4 cups sugar, warmed
2 tablespoons lemon
  juice
1/2 cup slivered almonds

1. Place whole apricots
in a medium bowl, cover
with water and soak
overnight.
2. Transfer apricots and
water to a large heavy-
based pan. Bring to boil,
reduce heat, cover and
simmer 15 minutes or
until apricots are tender.
3. Add ginger, sugar,
and juice to pan. Stir
constantly over low heat

until the sugar has
dissolved. Bring to the
boil, reduce heat slightly
and boil, uncovered, for
25–30 minutes or until
mixture gels.
4. Remove from heat
and allow to stand for
2 minutes. Add the
almonds and stir. Spoon
into hot, sterilised jars
and seal immediately.
Label and date jars
when cool.

Figs in Whisky

Preparation time:
  10 minutes
Total cooking time:
  35 minutes
Makes about 3 cups

500 g dried figs
1 1/2 cups strong cold
  tea
1/2 cup whisky or dark
  rum
1 cinnamon stick
1/4 cup soft brown
  sugar, firmly packed
1 lemon
1 orange

1. Place the figs, tea,
whisky and cinnamon
stick in a large heavy-
based pan. Slowly bring
to boil. Reduce heat,
simmer 25–30 minutes,
or until figs are tender
and plump.
2. Stir in sugar. Peel
lemon and orange,
using a vegetable peeler.
Remove any thick

From top: Figs in Whisky, Quick and Easy Plum Sauce, Apricot and Ginger Jam

white pith and cut peel into thin strips with a sharp knife. Add to the pan. Simmer for another 5 minutes.

3. Juice the lemon and the orange. Add juice to pan. Remove cinnamon stick. Pour mixture into hot,

sterilised jars; seal immediately. Label and date when cool. Store in a cool, dark place for up to 12 months.

Toffee & Sweets

Luscious, hand-made sweets like these are simply irresistible. Tie them up in pretty bundles, or arrange in small presentation boxes. They will add a touch of class to your fete, and they make exquisite gifts.

Buttered Brazil Nuts

Preparation time:
  10 minutes
Total cooking time:
  20 minutes
Makes 24

2 cups sugar
1/2 cup water
2 tablespoons golden
  syrup
125g unsalted butter
1 tablespoon white
  vinegar
2 cups whole brazil
  nuts

1. Line two 32 x 28 cm trays with baking paper.
2. Combine sugar, water, syrup, butter and vinegar in a medium, heavy-based pan. Stir over medium heat, without boiling until butter has melted and sugar has dissolved. Brush sugar crystals from the sides of the pan with a wet pastry brush. Bring to the boil, reduce heat slightly, then boil without stirring for about 20 minutes; or boil until a teaspoon of the mixture dropped into cold water reaches soft-crack stage. If a sugar thermometer is used, the mixture must reach 138°C. Remove from heat immediately.
3. Using a wooden spoon, dip each whole nut into the butterscotch mixture. Place onto prepared trays to set. Store between sheets of greaseproof paper in an airtight container at room temperature for up to 7 days.

Note: Other varieties of nuts can be used instead of brazil nuts.

Chocolate Nut Surprises (left) and Buttered Brazil Nuts

Chocolate Nut Suprises

Preparation time:
  20 minutes
Total cooking time:
  20 minutes
Makes about 50

100 g hazelnuts
100 g cashew nuts
100 g almonds
250 g dark chocolate, chopped
60 g milk chocolate, melted

1. Line a 32 x 28 cm biscuit tray with greaseproof paper or foil. Grease foil with oil or melted butter. Preheat oven to moderate 180°C. Place nuts on oven tray. Bake in preheated oven for 10 minutes or until golden. Cool on tray.
2. Place dark chocolate in small, heatproof bowl. Stand bowl over pan of simmering water and stir until chocolate is melted and smooth. Remove from heat.
3. Sandwich together one of each nut with a little melted chocolate; allow to set. Dip nut clusters into melted chocolate to completely coat; remove with a fork, drain excess chocolate and place nuts on prepared tray. Allow to set.

4. Pipe or drizzle milk chocolate over nut clusters in a zig-zag pattern. Store clusters in airtight container in a cool, dark place, or in the refrigerator during hot or humid weather.

Chocolate Cherry Cups

Preparation time:
  20 minutes
Total cooking time:
  5 minutes
Makes about 50

250 g dark compound chocolate, melted
50 foil confectionery cups

Filling
110 g dark chocolate, roughly chopped
1/2 cup thick or pouring cream
2 tablespoons coffee liqueur
100 g glacé cherries, quartered

1. Pour a teaspoonful of melted chocolate into each confectionery cup. Use a small brush to coat inside of cup thickly with chocolate, leaving no gaps.
2. Turn cups upside-down on a wire rack to set. Spoon remaining chocolate into a small paper piping bag and pipe patterns onto a

sheet of baking paper or foil. Allow to set.
3. *To make Filling:* Place chocolate in small heatproof bowl. Stand bowl over a pan of simmering water, stir until chocolate has melted. Add cream and liqueur; stir until smooth.
4. Place a piece of cherry into each cup. Spoon filling into each cup up to the rim. Tap gently to release any air bubbles. Place a piped pattern on top of each chocolate. Store in a cool, dark place for up to two weeks.

Treacle Caramel Toffees

Preparation time:
  40 minutes
Total cooking time:
  15–20 minutes
Makes 80

3/4 cup demerara sugar
1/4 cup treacle
100 g butter
1/2 cup condensed milk

1. Line base and sides of shallow 20 x 30 cm oblong cake tin with foil, leaving edges overhanging. Brush the foil with melted butter or oil.
2. Combine all ingredients in a medium, heavy-based

Treacle Caramel Toffees (top) and Chocolate Cherry Cups

pan. Stir over medium heat without boiling until sugar has completely dissolved. Bring to boil then reduce heat slightly. Stir constantly for 15–20 minutes, until the mixture turns a dark caramel colour.

3. Pour mixture into tin; smooth surface. Mark into squares with a sharp, flat-bladed knife. Leave on a wire rack to cool. When toffee has completely set, break into squares.

Note: Store in airtight container in a cool, dry place for up to three weeks. Refrigerate in warmer weather.

45

Mixed Chocolate Truffles

Preparation time:
  15 minutes
Total cooking time:
  5 minutes
Makes 30

200 g dark chocolate,
  roughly chopped
30 g butter
2 tablespoons thick or
  pouring cream
1¹/2 cups crushed
  chocolate wafer
  biscuits
2–3 teaspoons dark
  rum
2–3 teaspoons Kirsch
100 g dark chocolate,
  grated
100 g white chocolate,
  grated

1. Melt chocolate, butter and cream in a small pan over low heat, stirring until chocolate has melted and mixture is smooth.
2. Add crushed wafers and stir gently to combine. Divide mixture into two bowls. Add rum to one bowl and Kirsch to the other and mix each well. Refrigerate for 5–10 minutes, or until mixtures are firm enough to shape.
3. Shape balls from each mixture, using 2 level teaspoons for each ball. Roll rum truffles in grated dark chocolate and Kirsch truffles in grated white chocolate. To store, place in confectionery cases between sheets of greaseproof paper in an airtight container. Store in refrigerator for up to two weeks.

Note: Truffles may be rolled in combined grated chocolate and sifted cocoa powder.

Golden Honeycomb

Preparation time:
  10 minutes + 1¹/2
  hours setting
Total cooking time:
  20 minutes
Makes about 28 pieces

1¹/2 cups sugar
¹/4 cup liquid glucose
1 tablespoon golden
  syrup
¹/2 cup water
2 teaspoons
  bicarbonate of soda

1. Line the base and sides of a 28 x 18 cm shallow oblong tin with foil. Brush foil with melted butter or oil.
2. Combine sugar, glucose, syrup and water in a large, heavy-based pan. Stir over medium heat without boiling until sugar has completely dissolved. Brush sugar crystals from sides of pan with a wet pastry brush. Bring to boil, reduce heat to medium and boil without stirring for 6–8 minutes or until mixture just starts to turn a deep golden colour. Remove from heat immediately.
3. Add soda quickly to sugar mixture. Using a wooden spoon, stir gently until mixture bubbles and increases in volume and no soda is visible on the surface. Over-stirring will cause the mixture to deflate.
4. Pour gently into tin and leave to set for 1¹/2 hours. Remove from tin, peel away foil and break into pieces. Store honeycomb in an airtight container between layers of greaseproof paper.

> HINT
> Honeycomb pieces can be dipped into melted chocolate. Decorate with piped melted chocolate, if desired.

*Golden Honeycomb (top) and
Mixed Chocolate Truffles*

Rose Turkish Delight

Preparation time:
  20 minutes
Total cooking time:
  20 minutes
Makes 36 pieces

300 ml boiling water
rind of 1 orange
rind of 1 lemon
2 tablespoons gelatine
2 cups sugar
1/4 cup orange juice
2 tablespoons
  rosewater
red food colouring
3/4 cup icing sugar,
  sifted

1. Rinse a 20 cm square cake tin with water; line base with baking paper. Place half the water and the rind in a medium pan. Bring to boil, reduce heat and simmer for 10 minutes.
2. Combine gelatine and remaining water in a small bowl. Stir with a fork until gelatine has completely dissolved.
3. Add sugar, gelatine mixture, juice and rosewater to the pan. Reduce heat and stir until sugar dissolves. Bring to boil, then boil on low heat 10 minutes. Remove from heat. Add a few drops of food colouring. Mix well.
4. Strain mixture into wetted tin. Allow to cool and set overnight at room temperature. Dust icing sugar over a piece of greaseproof paper. Turn out Turkish Delight onto icing sugar and cut into 36 pieces using a flat-bladed knife dipped into icing sugar. Dust cut pieces with more icing sugar. Store in an airtight container in the refrigerator for up to one month.

Chocolate Caramel Fudge

Preparation time:
  20 minutes
Total cooking time:
  20 minutes
Makes 36

2 cups sugar
1 cup milk
2/3 cup thick or pouring
  cream
1/4 cup light corn syrup
1 teaspoon vanilla
  essence
80 g dark cooking
  chocolate, chopped

1. Line base and sides of a deep 20 cm square cake tin with foil. Brush foil with melted butter or oil.
2. Combine sugar, milk, cream and corn syrup in a large, heavy-based pan. Stir over medium heat without boiling until sugar has completely dissolved. Brush sugar crystals from side of pan with a wet pastry brush. Bring to boil, reduce heat slightly and boil without stirring for 15 minutes; or boil until a teaspoon of mixture dropped into cold water reaches soft ball stage. If using a sugar thermometer, mixture must reach 115°C. Remove from heat immediately.
3. Cool mixture for 5 minutes. Add essence; beat vigorously with a wooden spoon for 5 minutes or until mixture begins to thicken and lose its gloss. Pour into tin; smooth surface. Leave on wire rack to cool.
4. Place chocolate in a small heatproof bowl. Place over a pan of simmering water, stir until chocolate has melted and is smooth. Cool slightly. Spread chocolate evenly over fudge, using a flat-bladed knife. Leave to set. When firm, remove from tin. Carefully peel off foil and cut into squares. Store in an airtight container in a cool, dark place for up to two weeks.

Rose Turkish Delight (top) and
Chocolate Caramel Fudge

Hard Caramels

Preparation time:
  15 minutes
Total cooking time:
  15 minutes
Makes 49 pieces

1 cup sugar
90 g butter
2 tablespoons golden
  syrup
1/3 cup liquid glucose
1/2 cup condensed milk
250 g dark chocolate,
  chopped

1. Brush base and sides of a 20 cm square cake tin with melted butter or oil. Line base and sides with baking paper; grease paper. Combine sugar, butter, golden syrup, glucose and condensed milk in medium heavy-based pan. Stir over medium heat without boiling until butter has melted and sugar has dissolved completely. Brush sugar crystals from the sides of pan with a wet pastry brush.

2. Bring to boil, reduce heat slightly and boil, stirring, for about 10–15 minutes, or until a teaspoon of mixture dropped into cold water reaches hard ball stage. If using a sugar thermometer, mixture must reach 122°C.

3. Remove from heat immediately. Pour into prepared tin and leave to cool. While caramel is still warm, mark squares with an oiled knife; when cold, cut into squares.

4. Line two 32 x 28 cm oven trays with aluminium foil. Place chocolate in a small heatproof bowl. Stand bowl over a pan of simmering water, stir until smooth. Remove from heat, cool slightly. Using two forks, dip caramels one at a time coat. Lift out, drain excess chocolate, then place on prepared trays. Leave to set. Store hard caramels in an airtight container in a cool, dark place for up to four weeks.

HINT
If you prefer, the chocolate coating can be omitted and the chocolate simply piped or drizzled on top of the caramels. In warm weather, use compound chocolate—it will set faster at room temperature and is usually easier to work with.

Hard Caramels

1. Remove sugar crystals from the side of the pan with a wet pastry brush.

2. Boil mixture until a teaspoonful forms a hard ball when dropped in cold water.

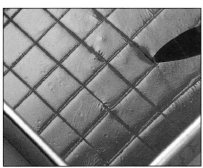

3. Mark mixture into squares with an oiled knife while still warm.

4. Dip caramels one at a time in melted chocolate, using forks.

Just for Kids

Colourful, fun to make and delicious to eat, these novelty treats are bound to capture the imagination of the young. They're sure to be top sellers at the fete, and make great kids' party food as well.

Cat & Mice Cakes

Preparation time:
  40 minutes
Total cooking time:
  20 minutes
Makes 12

125 g butter
1 teaspoon finely grated
  orange rind
3/4 cup caster sugar
2 eggs, lightly beaten
2 cups self-raising flour
1/2 cup milk

Frosting
125 g butter
2 cups icing sugar, sifted
2 tablespoons milk
food colouring
assorted sweets for
  decorating

1. Preheat oven to moderate 180°C. Brush two 6-hole, 1/2-cup capacity muffin tins with melted butter or oil. Using electric beaters, beat butter, rind and sugar in small mixing bowl until light and creamy. Add eggs gradually, beating well after each addition.

2. Transfer to a large bowl. Using a large metal spoon, fold in the sifted flour alternately with milk. Stir until just combined and mixture is smooth.

3. Spoon into prepared muffin tins, filling two-thirds of each cup. Bake for 20 minutes, or until cakes are lightly golden. Turn onto wire rack to cool. Spread top of each cooled cake with frosting and decorate with sweets to make faces.

4. **To make Frosting:** Using electric beaters, beat butter in small mixing bowl until light and fluffy. Add sifted icing sugar and milk and beat until mixture is smooth. Tint portions of icing in different colours.

Cat and Mice Fun Cakes and Crackajack

Crackajack

Preparation time:
  10 minutes
Total cooking time:
  30 minutes
Makes 9 cups

2 tablespoons oil
1/3 cup popping corn
3/4 cup soft brown
  sugar
90 g butter
1/4 cup light corn syrup
1/4 teaspoon
  bicarbonate of soda
1/4 teaspoon vanilla
  essence
1 cup roasted salted
  peanuts
3/4 cup sultanas

1. Preheat oven to moderate 180°C. Line a 32 x 28 cm oven tray with foil. Heat oil over low heat in a medium, heavy-based pan. Scatter corn over base of pan in a single layer. Put a tight-fitting lid on pan and allow corn to pop. (This should take no longer than 4 minutes.) When corn has stopped popping, remove from heat; turn popcorn onto foil-lined tray to cool.
2. Combine the sugar, butter and syrup in small heavy-based pan. Stir very gently over low heat for 5 minutes, or until sugar has dissolved. Attach a sugar thermometer to the side of the pan. Simmer,
uncovered, for 5 minutes or until the thermometer reads 120°C (hard-ball stage); stir occasionally.
3. Remove the pan from heat and remove the thermometer from pan. Stir soda and essence into caramel mixture. Pour over the popcorn, stirring to coat. Bake 5 minutes, stir popcorn, then bake for another 5 minutes. Remove popcorn from oven, add peanuts and sultanas; cool.
4. Break Crackajack into pieces. Store in an airtight container in a cool place.

Creepy Crawlies

Preparation time:
  25 minutes
Total cooking time:
  55–60 minutes
Makes 25

4 egg whites
1 cup caster sugar
green and red food
  colouring
liquorice and assorted
  sweets for decorating

1. Preheat oven to very slow 120°C. Brush two baking trays with melted butter or oil and line with baking paper. Place egg whites in a large, dry bowl. Using electric beaters, beat until soft peaks form.
2. Add sugar gradually, beating constantly until mixture is thick and glossy, and sugar has dissolved. Divide the meringue mixture in half. Add a few drops of green food colouring to one bowl and a few drops of red to the other and beat until combined.
3. Spoon each meringue mixture into a separate piping bag, each fitted with a 1 cm plain, round nozzle. Pipe caterpillar shapes about 8–10 cm long with the green meringue, onto prepared trays; pipe snail shapes with the pink meringue. Decorate snails and caterpillars with assorted sweets to form features. Bake for 55–60 minutes or until meringues are crisp. Turn off the oven but leave the meringues inside until they have completely cooled. Remove Creepy Crawlies from the oven and store carefully in an airtight container.

HINT
Caterpillars and snails can be tinted any colour. Use a variety of sweets for the features—tiny choc dots, or jelly tots halved, for eyes; cut up snakes for eyes and mouths; liquorice sticks for antennae.

Creepy Crawlies

1. *Cut each slice of cake into three rounds, avoiding brown edge.*

2. *Using reserved butter mixture, attach choc melt halves to each cake.*

Green Frogs

Preparation time:
55 minutes
Total cooking time:
Nil
Makes 9

450 g purchased
madeira cake
100 g butter
²/3 cup icing sugar,
sifted
2 teaspoons milk
red food colouring
vanilla or strawberry
essence
9 choc melts, halved
assorted sweets for
decoration (liquorice
allsorts)

Icing

3 cups icing sugar
5 tablespoons boiling
water
2 teaspoons gelatine
green powder, paste
or liquid food
colouring

Green Frogs

1. Cut madeira cake into three pieces lengthways. Cut each slice into three rounds, avoiding dark brown layer on outside of cake, using a 6 cm plain round cutter.

2. Beat butter in a medium bowl with electric beaters until smooth. Add icing sugar and milk, continue beating until mixture is light and creamy. Tint with red food colouring until pale pink and flavour with essence; mix well. Spread small mounds of mixture evenly on top of each cake round, reserving about 1 tablespoon of mixture. Trim edges of cake, tapering diagonally from top, with a sharp knife. Attach choc melt halves to sides of cakes with reserved butter mixture. Place cakes on a tray

2–3 hours or until firm.

To make Icing: Sift icing sugar into a large bowl. Make a well in the centre. Place 2 tablespoons of the water in a small bowl. Sprinkle gelatine on top; stir gently until dissolved. Add mixture to remaining water. Pour onto icing sugar and stir until the mixture is smooth and free of lumps. Tint with green food colouring; mix well.

3. Place one cake on the flat part of a fork. Spoon icing over cake, allowing excess to drain back into the bowl (make sure all sides are well covered). Transfer to a wire rack, using a knife to carefully ease cake off the fork.

4. Decorate frogs with lollies for eyes and feet. Carefully cut out mouths with a sharp, pointed knife. Allow to set completely.

3. Holding cake on the flat part of a fork, spoon icing over.

4. Decorate frogs with sweets to make eyes and feet.

Creamy Coconut Ice

Preparation time:
  20 minutes
Total cooking time:
  Nil
Makes 30 pieces

2 cups icing sugar
1/4 teaspoon cream of tartar
400 g can condensed milk
3 1/2 cups desiccated coconut
2–3 drops pink food colouring

1. Brush a 20 cm square cake tin with oil or melted butter. Line base with baking paper.
2. Sift the icing sugar and cream of tartar into a large bowl. Make a well in the centre and add condensed milk. Using a wooden spoon, stir in half the coconut; add the remaining coconut. Using your hands, mix until ingredients are well combined.
3. Divide mixture in half. Tint one half with pink food colouring. Using your hand, knead colour through evenly.
4. Press pink mixture over the base of prepared tin; cover with the white mixture

and press down firmly to even the surface. Refrigerate for 1 hour or until firm. Remove Coconut Ice from tin and cut into squares or bars. Store in an airtight container in a cool, dark place for two to three weeks.

Toffee Apples

Preparation time:
  10 minutes
Total cooking time:
  20 minutes
Makes 12

12 small red or green apples, very crisp
4 cups sugar
2 cups water
2 tablespoons white vinegar
red or green food colouring

1. Line two 32 x 28 cm baking trays with foil. Brush foil lightly with oil or melted butter.
2. Wipe apples well with a clean, dry towel. Push a wooden icy-pole stick or a thick skewer firmly into the stem end of each apple.

3. Combine sugar, water, and vinegar in a large, heavy-based pan. Stir over medium heat without boiling until sugar has completely dissolved. Brush sugar crystals from sides of pan with a wet pastry brush. Add food colouring. Bring to the boil, reduce heat slightly, then boil without stirring for about 15 minutes, or boil until a teaspoon of the mixture dropped into cold water reaches small-crack stage. If using a sugar thermometer it must reach 138°C. Remove from heat immediately.
4. Dip apples, one at a time, into syrup to coat. Lift out and twist quickly to coat evenly. Drain, then place each apple on prepared baking trays. Leave to set at room temperature. When set, wrap each toffee apple in cellophane and tie with ribbon. Toffee apples can be kept for up to two days.

HINT
It is important that apples are at room temperature when they are dipped into hot toffee. If they are too cold, the toffee will form bubbles on the surface.

Toffee Apples (top) and Creamy Coconut Ice

Marzipan Mice

Preparation time:
20 minutes +
refrigeration
Total cooking time:
Nil
Makes 16

200 g almond meal
1 cup icing sugar, sifted
1 egg white
almond essence,
    optional
32 coloured cachous
    (sugar balls)
16 currants
coloured curling ribbon

1. Combine almonds and icing sugar in a medium bowl. Make a well in centre. Add egg white, using a wooden spoon, and stir until well combined. Add essence, if desired. Turn onto work surface and knead for 5 minutes until fairly dry and smooth. Cover with plastic wrap, refrigerate for 10 minutes.

2. Divide marzipan into 16 equal portions. Mould by rolling into a round. Remove two small pieces for the ears. Roll remaining marzipan into a log shape, tapering the front to make the face. Place two cachous in place to form the eyes.

3. Make two small incisions above the eyes for the ears. Roll out remaining reserved marzipan and press into the holes to form the ears. Press a currant in position to form a nose.

4. Make another incision in the rear of the mouse and insert a coloured piece of ribbon to match the eye colour. Allow to dry out for two days. Store in an airtight container in the refrigerator for up to four weeks.

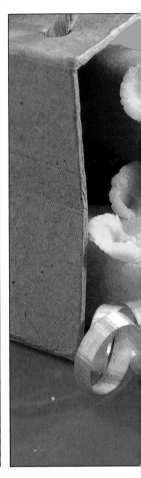

Marzipan Mice

1. Add egg white to almonds and icing sugar, using a wooden spoon.

2. Taper the front of a long piece of marzipan to make mouse face.

3. Press reserved marzipan into holes above the eyes to form ears.

4. Place a coloured piece of ribbon in rear end of mouse to form tail.

Rainbow Popcorn

Preparation time:
  10 minutes
Total cooking time:
  15 minutes
Makes about 4 cups

2 tablespoons oil
$^1/2$ cup popping corn
$1^1/2$ cups sugar
50 g butter
$^1/2$ cup water
2–3 drops red food
  colouring
2–3 drops green food
  colouring
2–3 drops yellow food
  colouring

1. Preheat oven to moderate 180°C. Heat oil in a large pan. Add corn, cover and cook over medium heat. Hold lid tightly, shake pan occasionally. Cook until the popping stops, then set aside.
2. Combine sugar, butter, and water in a small, heavy-based pan. Stir over medium heat until the sugar has dissolved. Brush sugar crystals from sides of pan using a wet pastry brush. Bring to the boil; boil without stirring for 5 minutes.
3. Remove from heat. Divide syrup into three equal portions and place in small bowls. Add colouring to each bowl; stir until combined and no

streaking is visible. Divide popcorn into three equal portions. Toss each coloured syrup through a batch of popcorn until pocorn is well coated.
4. Place popcorn onto an oven tray and bake for 5 minutes or until popcorn has separated and crystallised. Place popcorn in a large bowl, toss to combine colours. Serve on the day of making, or keep for up to two days in an airtight container.

Cone Suprises

Preparation time:
  20 minutes
Total cooking time:
  20 minutes
Makes 20

1 cup sugar
$^1/4$ cup water
3 teaspoons gelatine
1 tablespoon boiling
  water
3 egg whites
20 small round or
  square coloured
  ice-cream cones
assorted sweets for
  decoration
$^1/4$ cup hundreds and
  thousands

1. Combine sugar and water in a medium, heavy-based pan. Stir over low heat without boiling until sugar has completely dissolved. Bring to boil, reduce heat to low. Simmer for 4 minutes. Combine gelatine and boiling water in a small bowl. Stir until gelatine is dissolved. Add to sugar syrup in pan. Simmer for another minute.
2. Beat egg whites in a large bowl until stiff peaks form. Gradually beat in hot syrup in a thin stream. Continue beating 10–15 minutes or until thick and glossy and cooled; the mixture should have a pipeable consistency and hold its shape.
3. Place ice-cream cones on an oven tray. Fill bases with assorted sweets. Spoon mixture into a piping bag fitted with a 1 cm round, fluted nozzle. Pipe large swirls of marshmallow into each cone. Spread hundreds and thousands on piece of greaseproof pape and, lightly dip each marshmallow peak to coat half of peak. Place a piece of liquorice or a freckle on the other side. Allow to set overnight. Cones may be stored in an airtight container for up to two days.

Rainbow Popcorn (top) and Cone Surprises

Index

Page numbers in italics refer to pictures

Front cover, top row: Herb Vinegar (page 32), Caramel Slice (page 22), Toffee Apples (page 59), Citrus Trio Marmalade (page 34), Creamy Coconut Ice (page 59), Lemon Curd Tartlets (page 12), Buttered Brazil Nuts (page 42)